T0359722

SORCERERS AND SOOTHSAYERS
Friendly Street Poets 35

John Pfitzner received a commendation in the Max Harris Poetry Award 2008 and was joint runner-up in the 2009 Studio Prize. His poems have been published in *Studio* and in three anthologies including *Dodecahedron* (Poets Union Anthology 2010). In 2010 he co-edited *Season of a New Heart* (Poets Corner Anthology). By profession he has been a minister of religion and a publishing house editor. He lived for fifteen years in an Aboriginal community in Central Australia where he learnt an Aboriginal language. In his younger days he was an Aussie Rules player and marathon runner. Interests include human rights issues, reading, films, music and spirituality. He is married to Diana and they have three children and three grandchildren.

Tracey Korsten has been short-listed for the HQ/ Varuna Short Story Competition, has worked on the publications *Through the Opera Glass* and *Movers and Shakers* and has been published in the Friendly Street anthology for 2009. She is a public speaker, marriage celebrant, actor and director and is currently working on a screenplay, a book and a poetry anthology. In the past she has been a lawyer and a teacher. She lives in Adelaide with her two children.

SORCERERS AND SOOTHSAYERS

Friendly Street Poets 35

Edited by

John Pfitzner and Tracey Korsten

§

Friendly Street Poets

Friendly Street Poets Incorporated
PO Box 3697
Norwood
South Australia 5067
friendlystreetpoets.org.au

Wakefield Press
1 The Parade West
Kent Town
South Australia 5067
wakefieldpress.com.au

First published 2011

Cover artwork by Giovanni Cavuoto
Designed and typeset by Clinton Ellicott, Wakefield Press
Edited by John Pfitzner and Tracey Korsten, Friendly Street Poets Inc.
Printed in Australia by Griffin Digital, Adelaide

ISBN 978 1 86254 962 3

Government
of South Australia

Arts SA

Friendly Street Poets Inc. is supported
by the **South Australian Government**
through **Arts SA**.

fox creek
wines

CONTENTS

THANK YOU

to the poets who read at the city and regional meetings
and submitted their work for this book
and to the supportive and appreciative audiences.

Our thanks also to Arts SA for their continuing support,
which keeps our publishing program financially viable.

ACKNOWLEDGMENT

Friendly Street Poets acknowledges the Kaurna people
as the original owners and custodians of the Adelaide Plains.

PREFACE

Poets are the sorcerers and soothsayers of today. With their creative and skilful use of words they weave their magic, cast their spells and re-enchant our world. With their insight they alert us to portents, sharpen our awareness of what makes us human and envision for us a hopeful future.

More than nine hundred poems by over 160 poets were submitted for this year's Friendly Street reader. The poems were read at the monthly readings in the city or at one of the regional readings: Goolwa, Port Adelaide, Seaford, St Peters, Salisbury, Port Noarlunga, Tea Tree Gully, Murray Bridge and Flinders University. There was also a reading at the science institute, the Royal Institute of Australia (RiAus).

Reading poetry can be like dating. Someone catches your eye. You give them your attention, find out more about them, and, if the chemistry is right, you fall in love.

In editing this anthology we have chosen poems that have triggered our chemistry but also poems we feel will be alluring to others. We have tried to provide a wide and intriguing array of potential partners for you to meet – different body types, interests, age groups, backgrounds – in the hope that you will enjoy your dating experience, get to know lots of new poems and find many to fall in love with.

Twenty of the seventy-nine poets represented in this book have not previously appeared in a Friendly Street reader. A key aim of Friendly Street Poets is to provide encouragement for new poets and opportunities for them to have their work published.

Poets who took part in Friendly Street's mentoring program in 2010 are identified in the book. Under this program, selected people are given the opportunity to be linked for a year with another poet of their choice to help them develop their writing skills further.

In *The White Goddess* Robert Graves speaks of a poem being "a living entity" that can continue to affect readers with its "stored magic" long after it was written. We hope you will come under the spell of the poems in this book and will be entranced and enlivened by their stored magic.

John Pfitzner and Tracey Korsten

ALCHEMY

This year
we ran ahead of ourselves.

We became savants
and soothsayers

clairvoyants and prospectors.

We called to the future
and it came running.

This year
we practised alchemy:

out of love and thin air
out of hearts and blood

we made life.

This year
we couldn't help ourselves:

everything we looked at
everything we touched

turned to gold.

DAVID ADÈS

BOUDICCA

Wrong after wrong you committed upon me
from the day Prasutagus died leaving me without a son.

Did you think I could be subdued by a flogging
or by the rape of my daughters; that I would be

daunted by the mere weight of your numbers?
I am Queen of the Iceni, I am mother,

I am flesh and bone, grit and spirit. I live between
your thoughts, I itch under your skin, I possess

what you cannot take with your merely mortal lust,
your blood frenzy, your ecstasies of power.

I will not be dismissed or forgotten. I am practised in
the patient deployment of strength and the quick

riposte – the deadly flick at your soft underbelly
here, in London, here, in Colchester, and again here,

in Verulamium. The black I wear is a mantle over
the fire I unleash when moved beyond anger.

I will probe along the sharp edge of your lateral
for your weakness and you will burn. The rout of

your ninth division is only a prelude: I will be
relentless as a fly settling again and again

on an elephant's eye. You will have no victory
in my death – do you think your destruction

any less certain? My vengeance will permeate
through the centuries – incarnate in every woman.

DAVID ADÈS

I PAINTED

My sketches of the races at Flemington frightened you
as the hint of your husband's eyes were in the crowd.
You wore the lack of sun as with legs crossed you sat
on the second chair – the first draped by your skirt.

The second time you rested the morning in a wing-backed chair.
I painted you raw pink – your arms clawing the armrest.
Pink against velvet green seated on chair which rested on rug.
I painted as you stared towards the window's yellow light.

The next I asked you to shower – I painted as you stood
haloed by a window – the walls of the room apple green
the towels hung like robes and the basin a baptismal font
where your mystery washed from my palette.

The last time you slept on a bed in foetal position.
Your olive canvas somewhere between the Madonna and hell's door,
I painted your unusual jaw, your frown and pointed nose
and when you left I paid you the same as the week before.

GAETANO AIELLO

NAKED APE

Shedding the lanugo,
leaving the safety
of your uterine world
much as your ancestors
left swamp for land,
forest for open plain
you enter this world
as you must
clutching at air,
helpless
but for the wide-eyed trick
of eliciting love.

Tiny, naked primate – explore
sight, sound, smell,
taste, touch.
Set senses singing
(synapses wiring, re-wiring,
connecting)
re-invent fire, electricity within
imagine
make this world your own.

KATE ALDER

SNARE

All I knew about you
couldn't save you
all my wavering
between certainty and doubtful sound
all attempts to chart a safer course
just traps, lies designed to capture you?

Tortured struggle against your decline
fades to waiting, watching
passive as you fall
your voice forgotten
like the lost calls of extinct birds
only silence sings in the forest now
I too am lost
caught in my own snare.

KATE ALDER
Read at Port Noarlunga, September 2010

THE LAST POEM

I want for myself:
twenty hands,
a sheet of paper large as a tropical forest,
a pen big as a palm-tree,
a well of black ink,
to write my last poem
pouring in it my anxiety,
the paleness of children who exchange their school bags for
     beggars' tools, their toys for shoe-shine boxes
my last poem long as the night of Iraq
where I place the agonies of my homeland
etched on a guillotine's edge,
and the wailing of widows and bereaved mothers.
And read it from a pulpit atop a mountain
or from the electric chair waiting for my head's arrival –
before I begin death's slumber without nightmares –
bandages cannot smother my fires
rivers and rains can neither quench my thirst
nor drench my arid life
hand me the instruments of writing
I don't practise my freedom except on papers
let me die on my papers
let a poem be my tomb
I will have no tomb in my homeland
give me the tools of writing to dig up my grave
if not I shall begin my last sleep
but do not close my eyes
I want them to stay wide open like the door of our huts
like the hands of beggars
let them stay open
to see what is darker: my grave or Iraq?

For twenty years I searched in my home for my homeland
oh, if only I could gather the fragments of my corpse
my frequent moves between internment camps
and underground chambers of torture
scatter my memory throughout Iraq
for twenty years lovers in my homeland exchanged their letters
    in their dreams
and met each other only in funeral processions.

YAHIA AL-SAMAWY
Translated from Arabic by Professor Salih J Altoma

HAIKU

autumn
announces her arrival
with a flick of leaves

autumn sunshine
a burnished shield
face of evening

flight of cockatoo
the dip of branches
glowing with autumn

an amber sky
autumn settles the river
rounds the bend

MAEVE ARCHIBALD

THE SHELL

Fretted shell, cast like an ear
to hear the worried call of the sea
beyond a solitude
of dunes, hypnotically rounded

rhythmic as the wet horizon
swelling against the dreaming sky
folding it under song
that will not be located

This is a house that has no rooms
the inside-out that knows itself
losing beneath the waves
the certainties of words.

HENRY ASHLEY-BROWN

TAME SIBERIAN TIGERS
E D Rehorek 1932–2010

My mother could tame Siberian tigers
and really make them earn their stripes –
teach penguin choirs to sing colour harmonies,
there always was time for another story,
and tattoo a bamboo tune on a samurai-soul river-boat …

so she corrected the street-directory of the whole wide world,
my mother, who could tame Siberian tigers,
pushed those old reel-to-reels in several languages,
would not be a good little secretary, but rhymed instead
stack another bookshelf, fit in a crossword or three

run a quick drawing workshop before tea, gringos dingos
     fishes dishes
and really make them earn their stripes,
then rewrite that scene with the two opposing armies
mention satellites and mythology all in one
patch Hansel's pants and darn Goliath's socks,

but the Philistines want red noodles for dinner, promised
to teach penguin choirs to sing colour harmonies –
now the Spartans are beatboxing backstage someplace
and Jonah's playing solitaire, no sign of Hamlet
make some more petals for Esther, rocks for David,

and that whale's picketing the Japanese brewery,
and there's always room for another story –
like the one about the very last grandmother on Earth
or how there was a bunyip living in our bathtub …
so now she has a bus ticket to the Moon, one way,

hope she sends my regards to Hans Christian
and I'll tattoo a bamboo tune on a samurai-soul river-boat,
for now it's been raining here, but the trees are all flowering
they swim in the wind and there's petals everywhere:
just like my mother, who could tame Siberian tigers!

AVALANCHE

BLUE CRYSTAL BEADS

after Rupert Bunny's painting 'Madge Currie'

She had chosen a good dress
a pink voile sash
a matching ribbon for her hair
and she'd polished
her second-best walking shoes
until they shone
and while she was aware
they didn't match her gown
she wore the blue crystal beads
since people used to say
the beads brought out
the sonsy spirit in her eyes
and although her excuse
was that she'd sit sketching
at one with the mist and the sea
she sat waiting for him
because of his promise
when she might have guessed
or perhaps she even knew
that he wouldn't come.

Here on the dunes the sky is falling in.

ELAINE BARKER

OIL SPILL

Three men on the beach with shovels,
scooping up
fourteen thousand
barrels of oil a day

Ain't it the way

Mickey Mouse versus Godzilla:
the common fate made clearer;
this is the way the world ends.

Oh boy
greed and stupidity
rednecks who *always* know better than me.
Don't you worry about that!
Dead turtles, filthy seas,
can't happen here,
we're *rich*,
and we're *American*.

Ah but it's the US this time
not Bhopal, only poor Indians,
plenty more of them anyway,
nothing to do with US;
not far Alaska's melting northern coasts
out of sight and mind:
the underbelly of the US heartland.

Crestfallen people, so recently so proud,
like the royal spoonbills, smirched with oil;
Miss America fouled, diseased,
nevermore pristine, even in imagination:
the Black Plague in her wetlands
worming up through her guts
towards her liver, and her heart itself.
How have the mighty been brought low!

No pleasure I take in this, yet, dare I hope
something might be salvaged:
rednecks gobsmacked, *that's* something!
Maybe at least start taking the Apocalypse seriously?
Probably not.
They got computer games.

BRUCE BILNEY

DAYS

The art of days and unintended things
weeds piecemeal through to spring
jonquils and the sun in all the greens
and alyssum in clouds of white and
hardenbergia beginning; an hour lost
an hour gained and the brightness
of the morning suddenly gone and the light
of July darkening and in the lateness
of afternoon there are books come of age
come alive in the light of the fire, all the words
in-waiting foreknown and lying on the far side
of knowing and ripening like fruits.

KAREN BLAYLOCK

TOO MUCH MARY JANE

there can be too much meaning
I have trouble with the good green herb
because everything is so meaningful
red cars for example
or three objects in a triangle
words out of context from more than one book
also the CIA or the Queensland Police
who use that hoverfly to film me

but it is good, the green herb
taking a deep lungful of raspy heat
coughing and spluttering for the good cause
of another state of mind
a change of, increase of, consciousness
necessary
if we are to change the world anytime soon
I'll get around to it
just after I have this little sit down
in the corner with Jack Horner and my knees

I have found that if you smoke it
all-day-every-day for two years
meaningfulness
becomes a little hard to work out
as if something –
I can't quite remember
but if I could concentrate
and put all the clues together
I would understand

but right now I wonder
what those ants are carrying and why?

they know things

I would know things
if I didn't keep missing
whatever it is

BELINDA BROUGHTON
Poem of the Month, December 2009

MY COUNTRY

Beside a slate grey Massachusetts pond
I watch leaves of maple, oak and plane
summoned back to the black earth.
Trees that trust in a distant spring
shed life in a silent firework:
gold and scarlet leaves acquiesce
in drifts down the byways of heaven,
and naked branches, knotted-thumbed,
arthritic-fingered, farewell a fading sky.
Yet here, in this hushed perfection,
unspoken words come: this is not my country.

Back in my own country I know the names
of politicians, actors, the makes of cars,
know my bank PIN and my internet password,
when the news comes on and the garbage goes out.
But I do not know the red ribbing of my country,
the lay of valleys, the course of creeks.
I do not know each leaf, root, seed, fruit,
have never chewed a roasted grub or moth,
bitten the sweet of a honey ant,
stirred the wallaby stew.

All these things I do not know, as I could know,
as perhaps I should know, of my country.
But yet as I stand by this grey lake,
with all the leaves settling into the sombre
green of these dank northern woods,
I know that this is not my country.
Here I know my country is my country.

LARRY BUTTROSE

EYES OF REASON

I thought your eyes black
irises deeper than chocolate
drawing
allowing me to bathe naked
but today they're light
hazel
as you speak of sorrow
I reach up
touch your shoulder
realise my own eyes are black
I smile
we're each other's pupil
and you return
the mirror
of my desire.

JULIE CAHILL
Read at Port Noarlunga, September 2010

EULOGY TO A WARRIOR

On the tragic death of John Graham

John, was it ticking inside you
those days we laughed
in a war we were cursed for?

The toxins of a slumbering snake
leaked into your innocent veins
the deadly legacy of an aerial spray.

Did your body know
when we laid our Claymore ambushes
the tumor lay, stillborn, behind your eyes?

You were vital, John
as you fought for a truth long denied
by governments that broke their promises.

Thousands followed your dream of "a fair go"
only to mourn the loss of you
and of the rights you so gamely pursued.

Vietnam was never our nemesis, John
only the politicians who smilingly waved goodbye
and the people who scorned us when we returned.

KARL H CAMERON-JACKSON

SHOWER

There's something terrifying
though it's not the chair
or the thought of water.

It's that I've been manhandled here,
on a morning like
too many late nights.

My bad arm pinned close in a makeshift sling.
They boss the other
with soap and flannel.

Then lift me for the parts
that haven't seen the light of day
for near a week.

The nurse is stern, abrupt; cruel,
she admits, to be kind
because so many don't make it back.

Instead of her, Leana dries me,
with two towels, scruffily,
like a wet dog.

I savour this
more private attention.
Bask in her tender-rough touch.

AIDAN COLEMAN
Read at Goolwa, April 2010

ARROW

The way your slender-lovely neck
is revealed by your
    taken-up hair.

How, when the bliss-cloud
passes over, I lose the
    thread of where.

Because of your angel and mine
you wound with such
    exquisite care.

AIDAN COLEMAN

WAR STORY

In the early morning she saw them enter the bay
three luxurious ocean liners painted battleship grey
carrying troops from far away to far away:
to where all the men went
and some never ever came back.

In the afternoon she stood in the sun
at the door to the doctor's rooms where she worked
knitting.

The troops released from the ships streamed
by in twos and threes
and some were invited to dinner.

Afterwards she had twins
(one of whom had Down's syndrome).

She went back to standing in the sun in the doorway, knitting;
her mother looked after the babies.

He never came back.

BETTY COLLINS

FOR ALISON

Alison Gent, 20.9.1920 to 13.11.2009
feminist and supporter of women's ordination

Jacaranda, you choose your moment
to bloom in glory.
With feet rooted deep in earth,
firm trunk,
arms held wide in blessing.

Your bells ring and flourish
in purple abundance.
With green fern leaves,
you draw white from clouds,
to complete the trinity
of feminist colours,
you feisty woman-tree.

You proliferate soft colour,
a strong, gentle challenge
to any overarching harshness
we ascribe as blue.

You Advent herald,
you flag of the now,
not yet eco-system of God.

DAWN COLSEY

OUT THERE

A half shadow in the rear booth,
cafe breakfast plates
cleared away long since,
she lingers with another latte
amid a nest of newspapers
opened at crosswords, half done
a gambit for two heads, perhaps,
while she eyes the door
as a sparrow might a crumb
because a friend met hers like this –
but no-one so far means shopping
must be the placebo, yet again.
She drains her coffee, checks make-up
with a postage-stamp mirror
primps tint and curl
before the mall's weekend motley
her best side to the light,
for even a glance may be the match
to kindle her day.

DAVID COOKSON
Read at Seaford, July 2010

EYES

Your eyes widened just a millimetre
lasered my armour of senses
& if your lips had shaped a single syllable
they would have split into scintillas
that stone I try to deny
but you chose silence
& I looked away
not to admit you had read my eyes –
guessed at the stone:
we never knowing how its sparks
may have showered over us
when, eyelashes almost touching,
we merged.

DAVID COOKSON

THE SAME

we are the same
I look different

we speak the same
I sound different

we feel pain
I am the same

we need food
my food is different

we all love
I am the same

all have a home
my house is different

I am not white
we are the same

DOROTHY CORMACK
Read at Port Noarlunga, September 2010

A GOOD DAY'S PLAY

In the sixties
my father drove
my mother, my brother and me
to the beach house,
the car filled with
friction
and anticipation.

We'd stop occasionally
along the way
so my brother
could clip his crystal set
onto fence wires
to get the cricket score.

And later
on days that were too hot
for stifling
in the fibro house
we'd park under the pines
beside the local oval
and picnic to the sound
of cricket commentary.

Someone celebrated a century,
someone sat on a hat-trick,
pigeons invaded the pitch
and the guys in the commentary box
ate Mrs Someone-or-Other's
homemade cake.

Under those sighing pines
we waited out the weather
of my father's temper.

For once, together,
for once, united.
Hoping for
a satisfactory score:

four out,
tea at three,
stumps at six o'clock,
then home
(with no-one retired hurt)
after a good day's play.

JUDY DALLY

LOVE'S FLEETING GLANCE AND THE SLOW DECLINE

A memory lies where you once did,
where your form crept into bed and reclined.
A fleeting conversation your skin shared with my sheets.
Today we met in the street, face to face
and I reached to touch the clenched fist your white fingers formed,
held in close to your thigh.
You looked everywhere but at me.

What were frozen words have become a glacier,
a slow pursuit of sorts.
We watch its advance,
removing ourselves from the self.
The ache of pressure beats upon our skins
and so we turn our backs to the cold.

I pull back my hand and turn my face to the sky.
Clouds are flocking so I shuffle my feet to leave.
My back to you and walking,
our meeting in the street seems no more than breath across
    my neck.
But beneath this layer of skin
only I know your fingerprints on this pulse
are still red.

SARAH DALY
Read at Port Noarlunga, September 2010.
Poem of the Month, September 2010

THE FIRST THING I NOTICE

is the shared garden strewn with washed clothes and the carpet on the concrete with the chairs set out as if for tea. He is bustling from basket to line with even more clothes he's brought here from charity shops in LA and plans to post back to his family in Peru for them to sell, make a few *soles*; him bearing exorbitant charges for freight; money he doesn't realise or want to realise he doesn't have; now my mother's gone. On your own the pension's more, but less than two incomes the household used to survive on; even small incomes are incomes and one pension doesn't go as far as it might. More than it does in Peru, of course, where there is no social security to dream of, or jobs, real jobs, where everyone is a hawker or an odd-jobs-man, eking out existence-level livings in places we might call hovels. He is obviously not coping and the trip back after the funeral has made it worse, caught between two worlds, or three, when you factor the US into the equation. He gatling-gun talks about his kids and his brothers who want him out here, still sending money home, and his cousin with three houses, two in Boston and one in Puerto Rico, and you have to wonder, where can he fit in? He's not managing the place without her here and has taken to living outdoors and sleeping in the garage. All manner of things are outdoors: the portrait of my brother; door hinges; flyscreens; photos of his aged mother; of my mother years ago when she met his mother; of people at my mother's wake. We find a chest of drawers with the drawers upended and the contents in the front lobby where other residents have to thread their way through. They're not hacking it, are calling us; threatening legal action for his eviction. He's been playing loud music through the night, drumming his drum, and knocking on the doors of the single women, in the dark, and more. Of course they're scared. I am too. This gentle fellow who for years has kicked soccer balls to my kids: this man today we are coming to take away and commit.

KATE DELLER-EVANS
Read at Flinders University, November 2010

THE ELEVENTH HOUR
November 11th

I stop in the cold air,
lower my head.
The girl in the short skirt
unpacking cartons stops too,
and others move more slowly,
for seeing us.

I think of you both
in your watery graves,
unburied, unknown,
unknowing of what you gave
or why.
That was left to us to ponder,
parents, lovers, child,
gazing back,
still unable to fathom
all the tiny pleasures
and the pain of
living a full life with you;
and to have stood this day
together,
remembering others
and the ones still dying
behind the lines
and beyond all sense.

JO DEY

CHINESE GALLERY

It is cool here,
and silence seeps from corners
and behind the screens.

Twilight prevails
to preserve these objects
so long lost in darkened places.

Behind the glass
time is the exhibit,
the hundred, or the thousand years
since these works were wrought.
Centuries of mastery
in each angle,
in each slow curve
or wistful line,
a brow, a leaf, a fetlock,
or the garment's fall,
carries the imprint
of an ancient mind
that finds an answer now,
without translation.

JO DEY

HIDE AND SEEK

The children
play hide and seek
hide when the siren howls
seek dead bodies after

At the sparkles in the sky
people pray
make a wish
and let the dog off the leash

A mother says to her toddlers
the fireworks are coming
but the fear in her eyes grows
down in the basement
where the fairytales
smell of mould

JELENA DINIC

I WATCHED THE HYDRA SUNSET

A letter to Charmian Clift

"My darling Charm," that's what George called you.
That should have warned you, way back then.
To charm, bewitch, protect by magic, captivate;
a trinket having occult power,
that's what you were. Gave delight, excited him,
became the amulet for a golden god of words.

You hung around him, had his children,
lived as a peasant on the isle of Hydra,
your intellect and body an Aegean summer for guests.
Helped George with his writing, your own words
clutching memories of childhood by the sea
and your stern father on his pedestal.

You hated it when you returned:
the cooking, cleaning, shopping, the Sydney chaos,
work demanded by them all, pieces torn from you.
Through the haze of sex and booze, and pills,
hunger ate for recognition of your novels,
not the folksy column that brought in the cash.

You ended it. George coughed and bled
his way to literary fame outliving
his Charm's exhausted smile. Your name
but not your writing lingers
as the gossips wrench your reputation from its grave.

TESS DRIVER

JOURNEY OF THE PIANO

Karim Wasfi worried about the piano –
he had played Bach on his cello
with a gun by his side in a city
that still defies suppression
at the Martyr's Cafe in Baghdad.

The American pianist Llewllyn Kingsman Sanchez-Werner
drove in an armoured SUV to the Green Zone.
A ninety-member Iraqi orchestrea reached security
and one hundred and twenty minutes later entered.

The rehearsal space for the Steinway Grand stayed empty.
Wasfi and Sanchez-Werner hummed,
practised on an instrument with missing keys
while piano movers, the Steinway on a truck,
followed detours, no-go areas, burnt concert halls
and at midnight reached the Rasheed Hotel.

Sanchez-Werner's mother with a black felt pen
coloured scratches covering the Steinway.
Iraqi television broadcast the concert
with the Rimsky-Korsakov's Scheherazade finale.

Above the post-invasion horrors through heat and death
music burst beyond it all. Wasfi declared
"music survives and challenges the obstacles to civility."

TESS DRIVER

THE EMBERS OF MARIA VAN BECKUM

This is to be the last time I wake
to the cries of innocent men accused of heresy,
driven mad by death of will, stripped of
all dignities that empower us to fight for life.
Oddly, as my final hours are upon me
this tiny cell feels like home.
The bitter wind sent by Norse gods
floods granite vents flowing fresh air into the grottos.
Arctic November air has inspired hope
that the very breath of Thor would take me.
Nature proves cruel by affording me an immune system.
Nightly I am kept alert in cold sweat from horrific memories
seeing my son die in my arms pleading innocence to the Inquisitor,
who did not like having his transparent conclusions questioned.
No matter how I was interrogated
nothing can quite subdue a woman like the loss of a child.
Now my malnourished self fears not a church willing to sacrifice
     the pure.
With diminished body mass I devolve into something unlike myself.
Haggard as I must appear, I know in my heart
this being has lived with pure intent.
If there is to be a final judgment, whatever presiding deity
(if there is one) would surely acknowledge my existence fairly.
For me, realising this, the present presents itself as hell.
Knowledge and logic lost in fire, never to emerge on Phoenix wings.
This world of wilful ignorance led by social climbers
as well as men who vow to find a place for every soul.
They are the self-appointed dictators of morality
setting divine law and editing heavenly legislation to further benefit
     the lawless.

They point at me with bloody hands, coming to conclusions
    without trial
setting an example of me to those who oppose dictatorship
sending a message that progress is not wanted
and logic should remain a fable.
This is a world of men who invent and re-invent God
not in their own image but in an effort to be god of something.
In saying so, I am my own god. We make our own world
each having individual power over fate's current.
Today I shall embrace my weak audience set upon my
    frankincense flesh
dignified and strong in hope my transformation
into cinders will spread an impressionable ember.
In meditation I welcome fire, basking in the warmth of nature
knowing it is mankind's tyranny over the elements that is
    responsible for my departure.
I go with head held high, not towards the heavens
but in dignity knowing I lived honest and unflinching.

ANDREW ELLERY

MORNING ARMISTICE

Morning pallor on a grey day
not a five cent shine
to the sun.

Bitumen hissed all night
trees tossed and tangoed
shuddered and split.

Navy clouds, blue with rain
surfed in from the ocean
racing on the wild wind
learning to scream.

The stones listened
moon listed and tried to find
a space in the cloud-tide rush
to quiet-light the gloom.

Morning Armistice on a pale grey day
of debris and displacement
refugees and leaf litter
surrender and detachment
silent and still
only a five cent shine to the sun.

M L EMMETT

HOT BOYS

Hot boys express emotion
in the resonance and width of their exhausts
in pipe dreams of measurement
in the rev and roar of super-heated motors
mixing spark and sensibility
in the sudden screech and stretch of rubber
marking asphalt and bitch-u-men
out there in the middle ground
where the road humps.

Hot boys light up the night with high beams
cruise the darkest alleyways of masculinity
challenging old men at intersections –
in their soft leather seats and euroneat boxes
of air-conditioned luxury and debt –
to pole position and the chequered flag of fortune.

Hot boys in cars that throb with bass notes
and bootylicious chick lyrics –
sung by black boys wicked in the zone
always bragging 'bout their bone
and how they make the bitch moan –
snarl abuse at walking women
fragile objects on the pavement shelves
shaped colour lost in time
that pass beyond their touch and reach.

Hot boys are tiny traces of an oil-rich mixture
trailing blue smoke in their wake
foot to the floor high stakes, top geared no brakes
as they snake round the hills and the hairpin bends
as they wrap tight trees at the crash, crush end
and the hot boys cool in the night.

M L EMMETT

FITS AND STARTS
For Kate

She is my make, my do.
When I am think, she dream.
No blue is sky unless she,
and under is no ground
without she gravity.

Go walk on swim as airy
with birding name-song.
That loose as cloudly falling
when she light on
is shape she actually.

Off and on
when I unmade, undone,
rescue come.
She is my is,
my make, my do.

STEVE EVANS
Read at Flinders University, November 2010
Poem of the Month, November 2010

BLACKOUT

The dark is sudden
and I am stilled.
The stove clock says
not even its usual zero.
Light retreats along its wires,
the outside coming in.

Then the house feels me
through my own fingers
as I query drawers and cupboards
for matches or a torch.

Doubting, I pull curtains open
to the outer world
as, doubtless, others do all over town,
each of us checking our invisibility
to confirm we're not alone.

STEVE EVANS
Read at Flinders University, November 2010

FUTURE SIGHT

He spins and he spins.

The air around him rents and cleaves,
curls and fractals, into vortex,
counter vortex, eddy, wake, slipstream,

leaving, diffuse, dispersed, melded
with reverberations of wind-light,
cloud-drift, oxygen barely inspired.

He spins and he spins.

In the absence of calculus, he discovers
perfect geometry: neither equations
nor proof of principle are required.

He discovers the past can be left behind:
hair oiled like boot polish, a blackbird
panting, beer-soaked hallway carpets.

He spins and he spins.

There is nothing up his sleeve. No tricks,
no sleight of hand, no crystal ball. While we
see mere skin, sweat, taut muscle glow,

he sees his shadow depart, he sees a fragment
of his future, the suspense, the treachery of flight,
the denouement of safely negotiated landfall.

IAN GIBBINS

DEAD DOG (SUBTITLED)

No, not yet,
not as long as we are counting dog years
(or blue moons, faded, desaturated, pale
almost to transparency, almost to the sky's limit,
calling us to howl at the very end of space).

When spring tides peak
high at two metres, two point five, two point six
(it's that kind of day when land's edge slides
away from footfall, folded back through wavelets,
abating sea breezes, unfurled sailcloth echoes).

Until ten
in the morning, dogs may run on the beach
(off the leash, should we so desire, should we
be overtaken by the urge to race, to hunt, to dig
and scratch and roll, to dive, or jump up and fly).

As long as we
are counting dog years, there still might be time
(to learn one more new trick, to continue to breathe
ozone sunrises in old and familiar company, still time
to glimpse another blue moon, just before she scuttles).

IAN GIBBINS

DANCE OF THE DRAGONFLY
(Green Darner)

lady dragonfly
with your blouse of green lame
& your shimmering skirt of blue

in the sunshine
your gossamer wings remind me
of leadlight glass in church

you skim the surface of water
in your elegant ballet
often coupled

with a partner
& together you dance
a wild fandango

as you zoom and ski
across the pond together
in a grand finale

JILL GOWER

HIS AQUATIC UNIVERSE

he was one in the beginning
swimming in warm saline
love as neutral as creation
feeling eternity on his finger buds
treading the tepid pond
everything was only everything
there in the beginning

a muted emotion shaped his world
dull and cottonwool soft
he dreamed a salmon
pink twilight
his aquatic universe
a revolving harmony
with a hinge to something more

JUDITH HAINES
Read at Goolwa, April 2010

HAIKU

on the low tide
the moon rides on ripples
of water and sand

SIMON HANSON

Just one endless dance
trembling and moving bodies
sea inside our skin

LIDIJA ŠIMKUTĖ

in the headlights
an owl's last flight
twilight chill

BETT ANGEL-STAWARZ

Autumn evening
shadows stretching like cats
snatch up the sun

JULIA WAKEFIELD

POETIC JUSTICE
OR IS DEATH SO PHYSICALLY IMPOSSIBLE NOW MR HIRST?

Today in a tragic example
of art imitating art
the artist Damien Hirst
was dismembered and eaten
by a female tiger shark (*Galeocerdo cuvieri*).

Interviewed later by Sister Wendy Beckett
she was asked
Is this really art?
I put it to you madam
you are simply a large pelagic predator
with a walnut-sized brain
and your so called art
is merely a response to
a natural imperative
with no aesthetic merit whatsoever?

The artist replied
look, I'm a performance artist
I leave commentary to critics
applause to audience
I would add, however
that it was him or me
and just how long was it going to be
before Hirst's medium
became the hunting of man
the wiliest game of all?

She is reported to have twitted later
that he tasted
"just like (the artist) seal"

ROB HARDY

SESSION TIMES, PRONOUNS

a season of dying parents
our eyes take in the new light

exiting the cinema
an early drag

of cat tongue
long weekend

you hold onto your children
i hold onto my wife

she buries her father

RORY HARRIS

LEAF

autumn riot explosion & fall
this brittle fire
a bomber in a marketplace

RORY HARRIS

TANKA – SEED

Bathed first in red flames,
drawn gently from its armour,
the tea tree seed delves;
as my own heart takes first root,
freed by fire in your eyes.

ALEXANDER HENDER
Read at Flinders University, November 2010

CAUTION – THIS OFFICE MAY DAMAGE YOUR HEALTH

It's the tearoom gossip that irks ya
It stings and blinds ya
with its "he said" and "she said"
and "you'll never guess" and the bloody
"Oh my God! Oh my God!"
"What was she thinking?"
You thought at first they were all drab and grey
but it turns out the place is like a Bangkok brothel
It's the tearoom gossip that irks ya

It's the mobile phone ring tones that needles ya
They frazzles and dulls your brain
bleating from unattended desks
tinny tones of the latest TV soap theme
or over and over again some comedy show catch phrase
possibly mildly amusing the first time
irritating the second and then increasingly exasperating
until you swear you'll bring a sledgehammer in tomorrow
and smash the bloody thing to smithereens
It's the mobile phone ring tones that needles ya

It's the meetings that drives ya to distraction
They numbs and deadens ya
the "purely for decorative purposes" agenda
the action items never to be actioned
the head-spinning pointless Powerpoints
with ballistic bullets and apoplectic arrows
as meaningless as a mission statement
and sleep-inducing presenters talking to the wall
It's the meetings that drives ya to distraction

But it's the clichés that finally does ya head in
They blisters and rips ya
as you're listening to a heads up about world's best practice
getting incentivised to leap from behind the 8 ball
through a 24 by 7 window of opportunity
into a whole new ball game on a level playing field
moving forward, at the end of the day, in this rapidly changing
    globalised environment
Yes it's the clichés that finally does ya head in

MIKE HOPKINS
Read at Goolwa, April 2010

LOVE POEM FOR PLUTO

they say Pluto is no longer a planet
that it got too big for its boots
but those boots looked good on her calves
and those calves looked good in my hands

and we sat small in the night,
my body cupping hers, a boundary to the dark unknown
her fingers in orbit around mine
our lips spinning away from our cider to collide in the night

she stole words through the dark
to offer me a share of her slumber
and I drifted away full of stars

left her asleep, unknown
trailed my own cheek down to stardust

and … where were we both in the morning?
writing love songs to the moon?

INDIGO

THIS IS NOT A SOCIAL JUSTICE POEM

because it isn't socially just for me to stand
and be given a microphone and limitless free speech.
Though it isn't just social either.

It's just that with all this society
we could be more just about it;
make clear distinctions and dissertations
in public forums
about how rights exist more-so as wrongs,
about how well-meaning words
can never beat a bitten tongue when it comes to
mouthing the effects of persecution.

This is not a social justice poem,
because it isn't socially just for me to stand here
with one microphone, one story
and limitless free speech,
while other people, in other places
swallow their tongues to stay alive.

For their sake, please,
pretend you weren't listening.

INDIGO

ON POPENDETTA SANDS

He has a soft, stately shuffle
collecting the dust
on feet brown as the earth beneath

The natural strum of the guitar
reverberates through the liturgical intonations
(and) relics of a European past
omnipresent, in hard, ragged-edged hymnals
on Popendetta sands

The Marys are dutiful in choreographed ritual
holi-man dons the chasuble
as the yoke descends again
on Popendetta sands

An English restraint chokes the movement, the sway
the broad smiles reserved for some later time
when boats take the choppy seas once more
when talk turns to the latest arrival
perhaps something unexpected (less enduring)
on Popendetta sands.

GEOFF JOHNSTON

AFTER FINDING A 1953 MUSIC MANUSCRIPT BOOK

Thinking of Arnold Matters and acknowledging
'At night' by Sergei Rachmaninoff

I'm back in the front room
of that grey neo-Gothic building –
the Elder Conservatorium.

In front of me, near the piano
is that quietly spoken teacher
holding a lighted candle.

He is teaching me control
helping me to keep shoulders down
and be at rest upon the earth.

If I follow where he leads
he will lift me from the ground
let me discover what it means to fly.

I must train my tongue
to lie relaxed, keep my larynx down
and free the pathway for air.

I read his notation, try the scales
remember the sounds and rhythms
he wrote out for me to learn.

And as I learn to linger above that candle
keeping that glowing flame gently alive
I must let that breath come as a sigh.

My breath come as a sigh –
if I practise he will take me
to that world of German lieder.

I might be given the key to
a garden perfumed with linden trees or hear
a name float on the silent breath of night.

All this if my breath comes as a sigh
all this if I practise and if I practise
I'll move a long way from jackboots and rage.

ERICA JOLLY

TO MAKE SCIENCE MARVELLOUS

Let the square on
the hypotenuse come
as more than rote learning.

Let it come to us with
the music of the spheres
and Pythagoras' life.

Let the language of
trigonometry speak
of ancient pyramids.

Let someone explain
why Maxwell's equation
is seen as beautiful.

Let Sophie Kovalevsky
have an honoured place here –
not just a crater on the moon.

ERICA JOLLY

THE PORT

the smell of sea
and frangipani
my unique river
has a night life
few would believe

a blanket down
with breeze
that tussles hair
like hands
across a scalp

a rod and bait
a cheapish cabernet
my boom box tuned
to triple j

as nearby
dolphin pod herd
school of fish
for feed and
where water dapples
to reflection
of moon
and universe

ALAN P KELLY

WASH-DAY POCKETS

A rubber band
Two silver screws
A rusty cigarette lighter
One green marble
Plastic wrap with cake crumbs
from recess

A love heart stamp
A five cent piece
Watermelon lip gloss
Two fluoro hair ties
One long thick horse hair

Two business cards
One ballpoint pen
A slip of paper
A phone number
A woman's name

SHARON KERNOT
Read at Tea Tree Gully, September 2010

BOOKS

Towers of them
one on one bedside table
one on the other
twenty or thirty high
collecting dust and growing daily
like two skyscrapers
building their way upwards.

I lie in the shadows
of poets and poems
fiction writers and memoirists
and dream
I am suspended
between these stacked worlds
of words.

I make my way from one
literary structure
to the other
while the city lights
wink below
and cars and people travel
the dark roads home.

I peer into bright windows
full of metaphor and simile
and admire the construction
of plot and character
while my own writing convictions
cling to a precarious tightrope
of possibility.

SHARON KERNOT
Read at Tea Tree Gully, September 2010

FLOWERS

today I will try
to defuse a bomb

the one ticking somewhere
between your heart and genitalia

I will do it blindfolded

as not to see the damage
or fallout created

outside your bedroom I wait
with a bunch of funeral flowers

and my mini screwdriver kit

JULES LEIGH KOCH
Read at Port Noarlunga, September 2010

ON MY THIRD ATTEMPT AT LEAVING HER

about us
the morning is unpacking itself

as shadows are being swept
beneath furniture

through our bedroom window
the warm sunlight has ransacked
her body
I put

what I can
of this moment
in my pockets

and leave beside her
my words
unmade

before closing
so delicately
her front door

while around me
the sky has shattered like glass.

JULES LEIGH KOCH
Read at St Peters, August 2010

OWEN'S BIRTHDAY

At the going down of the sun
I sat in the Memorial Park in Sandakan
and wept
my son next to me – 13 today
mazel tov!
born on this day we acknowledge
lest we forget
I could never forget it
my first-born, my son
one half of the greatest love of my life
and greater love knows no woman
nor man
yet they were not men
not really
they were boys
barely older than my bar mitzvah boy
the age of my stepson back home
feeding my spoilt cats
whilst I indulge in this holiday
their day of birth
was their own mothers' day of remembrance
and in the morning
they would have remembered them
and little else
I think, too, of the Japanese boys
who committed these atrocities
the years will condemn them
yet each of them
was someone's son

they shall not grow old
they grew old enough
in this place
at that time
age did not weary them
war did
and we who are left
must enjoy growing old
celebrate each birthday with abundant praise
embrace the weariness
that comes from lives well lived
eat cake, say "mazel tov", cry, laugh, remember, forgive
but never forget
happy birthday
to all the sons

TRACEY KORSTEN

WHAT QUANTUM GRAVITY LOOKS LIKE

Time keeps everything from
happening at once.

* * *

Countless dimensions
will be needed to survive
the four we're lost in.

* * *

The universe duplicates
every time we look.

* * *

Time does not exist;
there is only more likely
and less likely.

* * *

There is not single now, now.
And there never was.

* * *

We feel a river.
In reality there is
only the ocean.

STEPHEN LAWRENCE
Read at RiAus, July 2010
Poem of the Month, August 2010

LOVE POEM

Reaching the ridge
we stood beside
the solemn rocks.
I watched you trace
the marks left long ago
by an ancient, shallow sea.
"Look down," you said.
Looking into the dry gorge
orange sediment and ochres
I imagined the subtle
sand-drift, wave-action
that changed forever
the ocean floor.

Like that sea
you have worked on me.
Subtly, inexorably
made your marks.
See for yourself
read them
with your fingers.

HELEN LINDSTROM
Read at Tea Tree Gully, September 2010

HOW DEEP THE DRY DEPRESSION?

A river bends, sluggish, dull banks exposed
where sandbars and snags craze dark water.

Peaches rot into saline soil while the blockie
loads a rifle alone in a desolate cutting shed.

Roo stew allays the hunger, a gnawing pain
as he watches her leave for work in the city.

A lead sky folds, shadowing rusty sale signs,
tilting to flood low orchards, weeping relief.

The blockie takes rod and reel to his landing
where a rapid tan river laps fractured pylons.

A midstream pelican casts a V wash to shore
going with the flow, to rise with grace, to fly.

MERYL MCDOUGALL
Read at Murray Bridge, October 2010

MEMORY OF A KISS

One frozen August afternoon
the sand stuck to our feet like icy dust
and cold, bright light
cast white sparks upon the sea.

On the shore
bare branches strung with fairy lights
opened spindled windows to the sky,

while the wind blew the living world away,
until there was just you and I,
the scent of salt and pinesap in the air
and the clear light wrapped around your hair.

MARGOT MCGOVERN
Read at Flinders University, November 2010

HIS FINEST WORK

This is the way the world ends
Not with a bang, but a whimper.
          T S Eliot 'The Hollow Men'

Breakfast was an abstemious affair –
tea and porridge, minus the sugar.
He'd been trying to rein in his belt
by another notch, pacing himself
for the marathon with an agile
electorate. And there they were,
as he padlocked his briefcase, all
clamouring for his sweat.
It was hard going, nose to the
grinding distance, the broken concrete

promises. By eleven, he was coveting
the calories he'd burned on his paper,
but plumped instead for a Barossa red.
Then it was back to the toil of signing
warrants. The first was for the arrest
of the municipal police stations.
And health, yes, there would be
axing, but he could stem the
haemorrhage after the execution.
Education, how easy, amalgamate

the schools and extrapolate the
difference after subtraction.
But your anxieties are misplaced,
he told the teachers. *I just mislaid*
a few calculi on my abacus.
And when the environment staff
told him they were dehydrating,
he assured them that artificial lawn
is so pleasing with its velcro veneer,
and so handy, there being no further

requirement for gardeners. Then
he remembered with a jolt that
his best buddy was Minister for the Arts.
But it was soon settled over luncheon that
the world would not end with
Thomas Stearns Eliot, and he'd heard
some excellent renditions of Bach
on the banjo. Three thousand warrants
later, they were a burden on his back.
He'd overlooked his fellow runners,

those worthy athletes would be
compensated. But the rest of the
proletariat could simply eat cake
if, domino-like, they collapsed.
That night, he was relieved to sever
the finishing line. *My finest work!*
he perorated, as he added the last euphemism
to his out-tray, then celebrated,
not with a bang of the champagne cork
but a click of the delete button.

LOUISE MCKENNA

HINDMARSH RIVER

Times when the river breaks through
and the sea, surprised, gurgles and sweeps in,
so that the two currents counter each other, merge,
murmur against the edges where we walk, just
past that single tree, its branches twisted and grained
a hunchback reaching out for air, tolerating salt,
a paperbark etched by sea and wind into a slow
dying defiance. I have to touch it, run my hand along
the bark, whisper to it as it whispers to me:
be gentle upon the earth, be crafted by wind
and rain, sea and river; remember what nourishes
the roots of your being.

KEITH MACNIDER
Read at Goolwa, April 2010

COUNTRY LIFE

I grew up in the bush
not the outback
not the red-dirt country
but the semi-arid plains
with mile upon mile of flat,
scrubby land
reaching out in every direction.

My family were farmers
so I'm no stranger
to the mulga and mallee
fly-blown sheep
or chipping Bathurst burr
out at the roots
with a hand-held hoe
paddock after bloody paddock.

And yes, I have to admit
I've shot at road signs.
Why? Because of that
great bush motivator: boredom.

Country life
can be so fucking boring –
the predictability
the compliance
the attitudes
and all the crap this brings.

I reckon that most people
who romanticise about
living in the bush

usually didn't grow up in it.
They never talk about
the melancholy
that is brought on
by the limitless sky and plains
or all the booze
used to dull this mood.

And nothing serious is said
of small-town politics
where, even in a place
with no more than
four houses,
a school, a silo and a pub
you'll feel hemmed in.

It'll feel too close
too small and too big
all at the same time.

It's funny though
if you're *a good bloke*
sometimes you'll think
it's a pleasant, friendly place
but only as long as you're
a good bloke.

This is the unspoken
dark side of mateship,
the mindless conformity
that it demands.

GARY MACRAE
Read at Port Adelaide, May 2010

SNOWFLAKES ON YOUR COFFIN

that year
spring came early
the almonds blossomed white against the bleak
then fell, like snowflakes
as did you
and all I knew was winter
I could not see the ripening kernels
nor hear the screech of lorikeets come to feast
I barely felt the stir of warmth
but as the last leaf fell
returning branches to the bleak
our child was born
and I knew spring

KRISTIN MARTIN
Mentored Poet 2010

VIOLET TOWN

Violet Town
The slow shift of clouds.

Barely a sound on this hot afternoon.
You could strum a guitar to an audience of none
in the main street under leaves in dappled light.
So quiet you can hear the distant approach
of a V-Line train long before the clang of crossing bells.

Such a pretty name on Honeysuckle Creek
once known as Violet Ponds
where streets are flower-named
an easy wind makes old branches creak
seed pods clatter onto tin roofs.

There's a weir somewhere, we've heard
but this is just a comfort stop off the Hume
en route from Euroa to Benalla
almost a mark on the Kelly Trail
famous only for its markets
hand-painted saws, home-made jams and Killing Heidi.

The inspiration for poems and songs
Violet Town – the slow shift of clouds
ingenious teens devising their own fun
summer days dreaming of oceans
as footpaths blister and crack
where silence is solid.

You can strum a guitar to an audience of none
in the main street under leaves in dappled light
so quiet you can hear the distant approach of a V-Line train
long before the clang of crossing bells.

DEB MATTHEWS-ZOTT
Read at Seaford, July 2010

ANTHROPOLOGIST AT THE CEREMONY

The tree hangs in the valley,
a teacher leaning over a student's shoulder.
Climbing out even a few feet
the ground swings away, distracted.

The trunk is fat and taut
making the sound of plapping
your palm on the warm belly
of a sleeping dog.

And once you are out there, suspended
amongst the clumps of eucalypt leaves
the tree holds out to the valley
like bridal bouquets,

you are above yet still of the vale,
privileged but connected,
the honoured guest,
the anthropologist invited to the ceremony.

Time is counted in the ticking of grass seeds,
you eavesdrop on the conversation of bees,
that congenial hum like the gossip of grandmothers
heard through a window on cards night.

Finches spark, the brown snake
recharges its coil, two existences
geared to travel the same day
at different speeds.

You lie, heart pressed to the trunk,
lungs and leaves partnered
in an intricate quadrille,
listening to the birds tuning their instruments,

able only to watch but never to know,
and in the breathing, the stillness,
imagine and find content
in the knowing but not the sense of kin.

The stars wheel out, the moon
who has seen everything, wonders anew
at the opacity of these familiar beings,
another anthropologist opening a notebook.

RACHAEL MEAD
Poem of the Month, October 2010

BLACKBERRIES

The bleached heat of February
hoardes a sweet centre
to the bitter fear of flame.
It is the month of blackberries,
a settler now
on the dark creek's bank,
in the valley's creases.

The stringybarks hold up their tanned arms
over this cascade of canes,
skimming the earth,
a flood of skipped stones.

Taller and more reckless
than my neighbours,
arms raked,
my fingers seek and pluck
blossom swollen into berry
hunkered back between barb
and suspicious leaf.

Later,
by the wrinkled creek
the torch-eyed fox
quietly
with tender black lips
eases ripe summer
straight from the briar
leaving bandicoot and flashing wren
in their knotted stockade
unassailed.

Full buckets gleam
with the lacquer sheen
of beetles.

Indigo fingered
and arms appearing fresh
from cradling demons,
I weaken into reward.

My tongue ripens
with black juicehoney,
the taste of naked valley
under wanton sky.

RACHAEL MEAD

THE PHOTO OF FORBIDDEN DREAMERS

I slipped from the queue ... the queue to death.

Before Kabul University's great hall
    on the steps to acceptance
    we stood, brothers in expectation
    of a better future
    for our Hazara people.

This one is gone ... shot ... my friend, Sakhim
    who spoke of truth and beauty
    who extolled a forbidden dream
    and entered eternity knowing
    there was no other way.

Ah, handsome Hadari, my delicate cousin
    he dances now, like rags on a kite-tail
    at the whim of a fickle wind
    he entertains the powerful
    who use him like a loose woman.

Ali Haider was studying law when
    his father ordered him to throw the stone
    bow to tradition, become a man
    punish her for losing her innocence
    but throw the stone ... he could not.

Mother begged me, "Leave ... leave now,"
　　veiling her reddened eyes, "escape this tyranny.
　　Your brother, my first-born, is lost forever
　　now you must go, my gentle son
　　you owe me nothing but your life.

"My boys, my boys," she moaned
　　pushing me from her into the darkness
　　of a dangerous passage
　　passed from kin to kin to stranger
　　shipped on a leaky boat over stormy seas.

We jumped the queue to life.

JACQUI MERCKENSCHLAGER

BEFORE BATMAN AND SPARROW

Rollers and breakers,
the restless ebb and flow of city,
drifted through dreams
in a Melbourne hostel.

Have others, camped by the Coorong,
used similar psychology,
heard thunder of hidden shores
as distant midnight traffic?

Before Batman and sparrow
did robin and reed-warbler
grace Yarra's untamed edge?
Did platypus slip down her tributaries
toward a pristine bay?

Before crystal condominiums
rose along her bank of bridges
that ferries limbo
and passing fingers brush,
which limbs draped their shading strands?
Which heads ducked under them
in barks, before barques,
before liners?

Were there river box and blue cranes
before docks and steel containers?

Before Batman and sparrow,
Indian taxi drivers with GPS navigation,
Caucasians with Angle tongues
and citriodoras bedded in median strips,
what trees were hollowed for nests
by beaks with sulphur crests
of lovers who dream
that this is normal?

MAX MERCKENSCHLAGER

MILK TEETH

I collect your milk teeth
in a small box for attar,
a mouthful of shells

that tell nothing of the nights
I walked the boards smooth
lulling you with my weary step

as your gums cut jewels.
Were they your tears or mine
stinging salty at my throat?

And only the seeping dawn
brought us ashore, you slept
and I was the wreckage

clinging to the damp smell
of ocean in your hair
wondering how not to drown.

Now, you spill from my lap
restless and graceful
and just beyond the thrum

of the tide that surged for you;
smiling wide just for me,
new teeth jostling for space

you are tumbleweed
showing me your sudden dance –
the handful of shells you found

like milk teeth in my pocket,
and me still wondering how
not to drown.

MOLLY MURN

ROADSIDE GRAVE

Just past the slaughterhouse a cross
marks the focus of one short life.

They say this one is a boy's grave. Mushrooms
circle it, knuckling up out of the blonde, dead grass.

The wind has a smell to it here, of old
blood rotting in the earth. The cross

throws a shadow deep into the field. I close
and open my eyes to it, to memories

of mornings waking to milk,
bacon and sun curdling in our tiny kitchen.

My bones shiver in this heat, wanting
to climb into the car and drive back to those years

when the child unborn protested with quickened
squirm, the ultimate discourtesy of life.

GRAHAM NUNN
Read at Goolwa, April 2010

SNOW IN MANHATTAN 1983

Unheralded
arriving on an indrawn breath
the first flakes flutter
randomly as moths
melting to transparency
on the warm windowpane.

Snow's first superstructure
space, spicules and crystals
elaborates surfaces
with light-filled embroidery.

But twenty hours later – a silent coup.
Reduction by addition:
angles obliterated, identity blurred
mysterious marshmallow mounds.
A landscape smothered without protest.

And the continuing snowfall
no longer seems innocent:
each driving crystal a tiny nematocyst
centrally directed to numb the quarry
into a millennial sleep.

SUSAN O'BRIEN
Read at Flinders University, November 2010

HELSINKI GOODBYE

We've spent this day sightseeing,
avoiding through tourism
the sense of being unclasped.
Soumalina, the harbour
Lutheran church, Orthodox cathedral
and Market Square.

At the end, we return
to the hotel room.
Float for a moment
on the crisp life-raft
of a standard hotel bed,
letting the currents of twilight
stream past.

But time compresses,
despite this snared moment
yelping in sudden pain.
I stand at the international gate
in Helsinki airport,
looking for myself in your eyes,
amongst the cigarettes
and stale coffee of a transit lounge,
tasting the acid
of airport goodbyes.

JULIET A PAINE

SANCTUM

I was running
          from hunger
& mercenary selves
I was chasing
          harbours in the sharp
          angles of mirror's
                    noses
          reviving bitter odes
                    to the lap
                    of her double

when I slipped
          into yr mind

Won't you let me
          hide for a while?
You won't even know
          I'm here …
If you let me hide
          for a while, I'll
          bolt the latch
          before I leave
you won't even know
          I've been …

& I'll go quietly

(when you've forgotten
          that I exist …)

& you won't remember
          a thing

ANTHONY PARMEE

GALILEO'S TELESCOPE

It could be just a toy
or the latest advance in military technology,
but when he aims it at the heavens,
the whole cosmos is shaken.
Earth begins to spin,
hurtling through space
in its race around the sun.
On the lunar surface,
mountains and valleys appear –
the heavenly bodies
no longer perfect and immutable.
Each planet assumes its rightful place
in its elliptical heliocentric orbit.
Jupiter acquires moons and Saturn rings.
The sun's face becomes spotted.
Stars retreat to unimaginable distances.
Wonders are revealed
more wonderful than those they displace
as old certainties crumble with
the authorities that supported them.
The universe starts divulging secrets
in the elegant poetry of mathematics.
People learn to measure, imagine,
experiment, observe,
and a later generation
sends people to the moon,
where a space-suited astronaut,
outside his lunar module,
drops a hammer and a feather together
and sees them hit the ground
simultaneously.

JOHN PFITZNER
Mentored Poet 2010

JUNKYARD DOG

I finally understand you
understand how your humanity has been decayed, degraded
into the dangerous creature you now are
you who snap and snarl,
savage those within your reach
Oh, junkyard dog
I keep my distance now
ensure my own protection

Once I thought it was simple
once I thought you were no more than a savage beast
until I looked again ...
            ... at your mistress

Ah your clever, clever mistress
it was she who called you savage
named herself captive to your rage
I pitied her as she whimpered of her fear
yet ...

I saw her fingers snap
her eyes alight at your discomfort
her hands rub themselves in glee
not knowing I was watching

Oh, once man
I crouched at safe distance
hidden from you both
I watched as she kept you

starved
despised
humiliated
as they do the curs who prowl the junkyards at night
behind locked gates
I saw how she knows your needs to deny them
how she goads you to savagery
brings you irresistible victims
to satiate your pain
I saw how she binds their wounds
with soothing words
and frightened apologies
their anger misdirected

They never suspect it is she
who required them mutilated
and disempowered
Oh junkyard dog
it is you who have my pity now

I tried to leave it with you
but you scorned me
mauled me
I retreated in defeat
with nothing but the crumbled remnants
of my unwanted pity
still clinging to my hands.

SUZANNE REECE

DOMESTIC JOURNALISM

This is domestic journalism.
I'm forcing it out like the rent.

I'm craving a blanket ... of crashing rains.

Come pulverise sad bits of junk.
Surround these temples of half-dead dreams all weathered with fear.

P-link! P-lonk!

Only soft, insistent, irregular rhythms count me down.
Out.
Let's face it, I'm beaten.

Cast a spell, disperse this gloom.
Some snake oils should do it.

Green-sea globules ooze slowly
through bromine showers with oily grace.

Like you once trickled ...
down,
deep,
somewhere inside me.

Lemongrass blades slash through mixed blizzards.
Acid needles rip through mud, stiff and honeyed

Ker-PLUNK!

Rusty old drums.
Dark back alleys of my deepest middle earth,
where you once illumined.

Still our dreadful winters darkened.
Sometimes tending tinder re-ignited.

Now cruising past me, merry way,
sneering lips, bruising resentments.

You spat in my potions.

Pound away rains ... console me.

PHILIP GILES REED

NONSENSE

she kisses like a shotgun blast through Hemingway's skull

a record skips
a record skips
a record skips

and suddenly
swans are reflecting elephants

geckos crawl up the inside of my eyelids
spiders hang their webs between the spaces in my fingers
beetles dig their burrows beneath the surface of my skin

snails are being accelerated without limit
allowing effect to be witnessed before cause
allowing time to be traversed
allowing those snails to go back through the ages
meet the ancients
and collect ankhs and dinosaur bones

meditations have opened
third
fourth
and fifth
eyes
they blink as one

too many poems have created a shortage of words
forcing parliaments to pass legislation declaring
henceforth
that all literary works shall begin with their
humble conclusions
and conclude with their
proud beginnings

battered, beaten and bored,
instruments have risen up
thrown off their masters
and have taken to playing in the streets

scientists and holy men have
armed hands with bats, bottles and knives
overturned tables
smashed chairs
and are brawling
to better understand the inner workings of karma

Nigerian Ministers of Finance have taken up residence in
Buckingham Palace
after Lizzie
signed over the British Empire
as collateral for a bad investment

Jesus has come back Iraqi
and now looks set to nail himself to a
question mark
while Romans sacrifice themselves
like Aztecs
to sacred Australian Idols

rainbows curl from buildings
while legless ponies stampede through laneways
and Rick from accounting
squeezes himself into a lift
crammed full of rhinoceroses

armless boys stare vacantly,
from park swings which remain stationary
at a position perfectly horizontal to the ground

people fall up flights of stairs
while flocks of airplanes travel south for the winter
to enjoy cocktails on Brazilian beaches

wordsmiths hammer and forge mathematical formulae
intent on calculating pi to infinity
thereby allowing circles to write
this very poem

and I come to realise that
everything between me and her
all of it
is a beautiful
perfect
nonsense

ROYCE

A NAVIGATION OF 90 SECONDS

from the first drag and throw on to its lower back
right foreleg clamped under the shearer's thigh
as he strikes a path along the breast blade
down to the udder
paring a deft path terror has frozen
to the nether parts – round the genitals
back up the underbelly to the chin
slicing blind – experience is the sole pilot
through thick creamy slabs – the sheep collapsed
in dreamy stupor as the buttery fleece falls away
then startles anew as the blade
rocking over bony brows
swoops in to the neck
moves round the head the ears the eyes
in dangerous navigation –
blood as close as a stray thought –
cleans up the ragged ends without a snick
then a swift roll of the body
to sail along the long spine
numbed by rhythmic strokes
relaxed for an instant
release – brief paralysis
then a blind scramble on the floorboards
scuttling to freedom – with blank eyes it
refocuses on the distance
forgetting already

ROS SCHULZ

WIVES OF THE WARRIORS

wives of the warriors draw curtains
across windows where nightmares hang
waiting for the darkened night
to spread black wings that circle
and swoop sharp-clawed
through thin layers of sleep

like sirens calling
they sing their soldiers home
from memories like quicksand
with soft murmurings they drown
the sounds of tanks and guns
war that will not stop

wives of warriors keep moving
boulders to fill craters
with bare hands they till soil
watered with tears
smoothing the surface of their lives
sowing seeds of peace

they stitch together edges
of flesh that tears
of wounds that weep
wash away blood that never dries
that seeps and stains each day
like purple dawn

wives of warriors know
the depth of the ocean
know the hard high mountain
that lies beneath the star of hope
the unseen force that tugs
urges them upward

wives of the warriors see
stories in each other's eyes
silent reflections of compassion and courage
know that they travel
the same unmapped way
heroines of long long war

VERONICA SHANKS

PLAIN LOCO

your mind is a gun. plain loco.
bent as a cigarette.

my heart bucks like a bronco
at the whipcrack of your name.

love floats in on a vulture's wing.
magnificent, raw and hungry.

i am caressed by your spurs
and cry into your whiskey.

in the darkness i hear your hot fingers
scrabble for my gunbelt.

and still i wait in the moonlight.
a herd of beeves to be rounded up.

branded. then smuggled
across the border

into the dark mexico of your love.

THOM SULLIVAN
Read at St Peters, August 2010

MOORLANDS

Here the wind
begins its gallop

across the hills'
grey hessian –

hurdling
the shelterbelts,

the brakes of gorse
and wattle.

Any beauty here –
any – is subtle.

This lungful
of musty grasses,

this low, grey
plain of cloud.

THOM SULLIVAN

KIRIAY

To strangers you looked harsh.
Hard angles and corners
that bent sharply
and twisted
like daggers into skin.

But inside you were soft,
rubbery and fluid as a bicycle wheel
dipped in dew on the front lawn
where we would sit
and count the cars that drove
in blurring colours
past our feet.

Your eyes, dark and
full-framed with lashes,
leapt at me like plunging shadows
through our late-night conversations
of whispers and hushed giggles.
Smoking,
fingernails painted black
and stained with ink, shaping puppets
on the walls,
you would tell me secrets
in muted tones.
My heart would flutter in the darkness.

There's silence now and cobwebs;
dusty recollections and a
hack-jawed cough.
In my mind I map your silhouette
and paint you back to life with tears.

ATHENA TAYLOR

MORNING

old man's cough hawks up from the pit / apartment subzero in prefabricated block / as radiobirdflight unzips dawn / a yawn brings empty relief / & movement lubricates / my lover glistens / sugared & cerealed / while i caffeinate cells / & coagulate / slowly toasting the abc news / as morning shoots its load / premature ejaculation of disaster / sizzling on the overheated frypans of undercooked consumers who / let's face it / just want to get on with their day //

JENNY TOUNE

KANSAS DREAMING

i move through the night
bursting the blistered sac of conformity
follow music until it erupts out of trance-dance
let the mushrooms play latino riffs
on this amazon moon, &
never underestimate the power of ghosts
even for a skeptic
there's magic that refuses to budge

dorothy checked out of this hotel years ago
believing it was all a sugar-junkie's dream
but i flung my red shoes into the river
found it's better to dance the vision
with burning feet
than to tiptoe through the glitterati's minefield
collared & sequinned like paris h
even for a dreamer
there's reality that refuses to budge

reality that slides into focus
like wood under fingernails
a caress
that allows exquisite abandon ...
there's no place like home

JENNY TOUNE
Poem of the Month, July 2010

MORE MUSIC OF THE NIGHT

I play your body like a violin
that has been left too long untouched,
recall to life the sound within
that, dormant, waited long, dry years.
Now, half-reluctantly, the body starts to throb,
at first discordant, scratchy, but with time
the voice revives, retuned by loving hands
and small and pleasing sounds begin again.
Until, full-throated, music pours once more –
I feel your body throb with life.
We move together, tempo quickening.
Andante is transformed, allegro takes its place;
con brio, feeling rises, and the notes sing forth.
Vivace rises to a climax, then subsides,
and music floods the room until at last
a languorous legato draws the movement
to a close. The strings are slackened
and the bow returns to rest inside the case.

VALERIE VOLK

BONSAI

We stand together,
evicted tenants of the womb now interred
under grey glazed stone and consider:
the arching branches of the stunted juniper,
its arthritic twist of roots searching the blue glazed dish.

She says in her little voice: "I wonder if it hurts them; if they suffer?"
or something about the imprisonment of these beautiful dwarfs,
whose methodical yoking yields this aching elegance.

And I think how *I* have thought this too,
start, at this connective tissue of thought and at our lonely
    sameness,
at the years of conflict and partings and still
this simple sameness like a script,
written in that watery space
where first I slept – then she.

MARIA VOUIS
Read at Flinders University, November 2010

SOMETHING TO TWEET ABOUT

Half an hour before midnight
a giant danced on our roof.
For ten long seconds
the world went insane
the air around us roared, the tiles tap-danced
the roof beams rumbled and rolled
the ceiling shimmied, the windows rapped
the dishes jigged, the walls jitterbugged
the floor waltzed, the dog screamed
the cat sparked and sizzled
and we stood frozen, listening
as our hearts stampeded.

Then all was still.

And then
we texted and twittered, blogged and bragged
chattered and joked, laughed and drank
and drank some more, and staggered into bed
half wanting to feel the exquisite thunder of
his giant feet once more.
He'd danced all over Adelaide, but only on tiptoe, here and there
leaping lightly over rooftops, thrilling us with the tender touch
of his awesome toes.

Last week a troop of fearsome giants
kicked and stamped a terrible tarantella
on a remote region of northwest China.
There was no-one left to twitter
blog, brag or chatter
no-one joked or laughed
at their savage death dance.

JULIA WAKEFIELD
Mentored Poet 2010
Read at Goolwa, April 2010

THE DOOR

of my childhood
is closed
locked
I've thrown away
the key
yet
she waits
in the dark
cold and alone

G M WALKER

SORTING

minefields of possessions
exploding time bombs
of memories and ghosts

G M WALKER

A BETTER WORLD

Money is mute.
Humility talks.

Landmines are consumed by
dung beetles overnight.

People have the confidence of cats,
the loyalty of dogs.

Every word is a dollar to be spent wisely.

Every child is declared a National Treasure.

Children conduct workshops for parents
on Spontaneity and Optimism.

Conformity is tolerated.
Uniqueness celebrated.

ROB WALKER

LINES WRITTEN IN HIMEJI, 2008

Each day I skate tectonic plates
the disconnect is now the norm
reality's a fracture zone
Guernica at junior high
the all-girl band at Kobe Quay
swings American Patrol
too young to see the irony.
I smile and share the joke alone.

And in the aisles of Bon Marché
Mulligan and Brubeck groove
like someone took the Books of Man
and Space and Time and cut them up
then threw the pieces to the wind
and they (and I) just landed here …

ROB WALKER

STEPHANIE ONLINE

Your voice flitters across my screen
and I am delighted
with the laughter in your words.
You make
a joke
you know I'll laugh at
and I do.

Your voice flits across my screen
as you teach
this old bitch
new tricks;
and we laugh out loud
in slang
lol and rofl all over the box –

and then,
the time difference
takes its toll
and you are gone

and I
go to sleep
with a smile
on my face.

SARAH WAUCHOPE

BETTER THE DEVIL YOU KNOW?

Husband's late; children cry.
Spuds aren't peeled; clothes won't dry.
Dog escapes; neighbour's cross.
Three-year-old thinks she's boss.
Fridge won't work; garden's dead.
Bills aren't paid; kids want fed.
One throws up; damn that phone.
Baby chews doggie's bone.
Screeching brakes; car in drive.
Fam'ly dog still alive.
"Hi there dear, hubby's back.
Swore at boss, got the sack."
Scruffy spouse, rarely here,
loves his mates, loves his beer.
Scoffs down food, burps and swears.
Never helps, never cares.

Handsome man, thinks I'm cute.
Winning smile, well-cut suit.
Very rich; car's divine.
Wants to share food and wine.
Spoils me heaps, oozes charm.
Luncheon date, what's the harm?
Think it's love; offers cruise.
Can't resist, full of booze.
Bye-bye kids, want to roam.
Dump my man, leave my home.
Life is full, lucky find –
sober now, changed my mind.
Back again, family life.
Just a mum, just a wife,
staying home with my chap.
Better off? That's just *crap*!

JILL WHERRY

PAST CONJUGATION OF THE VERB TO MARRY

I married
I married a white knight
with a slow horse
on rough terrain
I was the bee in his helmet
He would sleep in his armour
When he finally took it off
I saw his heart had been given to another
His cause was for lost love
mine for safety

Pearls and black roses
A bad omen they said
not knowing I chose, loved them
A curt affair
His genes, generations of bread and butter
mine of passionate, cruel stones
Forty-two degrees in the shade
sitting tensely in formals
cracking our Crème Brule
Driving from the church
he asked for the cricket score

You married
You married
noun not verb
White whipped candy, French nails
fake tan

Your mother on oxygen
Had to see her first-born
married, if not well
Under the tulle, her grandson
a happy family fracas
trimmed in lurid lace
She died anyway

How your milk
must have curdled
at the funeral
What will you marry next
to have her back?

He married
He married, as was the custom
A suit, speeches, the pressies
a day's notoriety
Lots of grog to loosen
a chain he already despised
The certainty of open
legs and ironed shirts
He loved his house, the kids
the car, the view
Lamingtons in the lunch box
Pre-wired for the burbs
But they forgot to teach him
the dangers of fantasy

We married

We married oil and water
decorative statements
odd socks, budget and actual
We married mismatched sheets
ends of roof joists
opinion and dissension
ideas of the other
We married anyway

They married

They married like they married before them
Lonely, bored, bedazzled by desire
Because part of them feels whole
inserted in the other
It is logical, ludicrous, popular
They married for the long plough
rocks, stumps and droughts
Taught their boys how to hate monotony
Girls, how to darn, clean and mend
They married for love of marriage
What God has put together
let no verb bring asunder

CARMEL WILLIAMS
Mentored Poet 2010
Poem of the Month, February 2010

For further information about
Friendly Street publications and activities please visit
our website: friendlystreetpoets.org.au
email: poetry@friendlystreetpoets.org.au
postal: PO Box 3697, Norwood SA 5067

§